# Foxes
# For Kids
## Amazing Animal Books
## For Young Readers

*By Zahra Jazeel*

**Mendon Cottage Books**

*JD-Biz Publishing*

Read More Amazing Animal Books

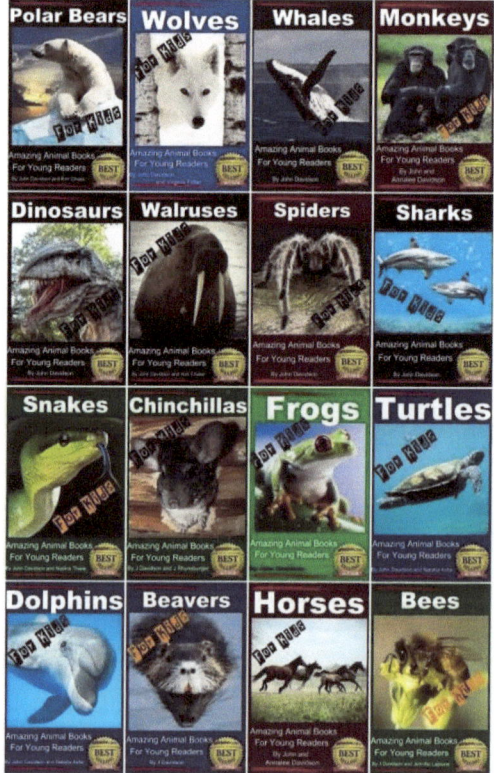

Purchase at Amazon.com

**Download Free Books!**

**http://MendonCottageBooks.com**

# Table of Contents

Introduction ................................................................ 4

About Foxes ............................................................... 6

Characteristics ........................................................... 8

Foxes in different folklore and mythology ....................... 10

Red Fox .................................................................... 12

Gray Fox ................................................................... 14

Arctic Fox ................................................................. 16

Fennec Fox ................................................................ 18

Kit Fox ..................................................................... 20

Swift Fox .................................................................. 22

Bengal Fox ................................................................ 24

Silver Fox ................................................................. 26

Crab-Eating Fox ......................................................... 28

South American Gray Fox ............................................. 30

Bat-Eared Fox ............................................................ 32

Hoary Fox ................................................................. 34

Tibetan Sand Fox ........................................................ 36

Author Bio ................................................................ 38

Publisher .................................................................. 45

# Introduction

Have you heard about the story of fox and the crow where the fox tricks the crow to drop the food from tree? I'm sure you most probably did. Foxes are portrayed as cunning and deceitful creatures in many stories and fables. But is it really true or just a myth? The foxes are most probably assumed as such because of their sneaky ways of hunting for a prey. However, wouldn't it be exciting to know more about these so call "cunning creatures"?

Did you know that foxes show a great deal of love, attention and care when raising their young? Let me recall an incident. It was May 2009. A baby fox was badly injured and was unable to move for he was caught in a snare for 2 weeks until he was finally rescued by the RSPCA. He survived miraculously because of the food his mother brought when he lay there trapped. Heart-warming, isn't it?

Join us as we explore more about foxes, their different species, habitats, behaviors and interesting facts like the one mentioned above. Now we provide you the opportunity to decide on the nature of foxes.

# About Foxes

Foxes are mammals belonging to the family of Canidae. They are omnivorous animals consuming both plant and animal matter. Their sizes range from small to medium depending on the species. Common features of a fox include long bushy tail, pointed triangular ears, flattened skull and a snout which is slightly upturned. Out of the 37 species present, only 12 are considered to be "true foxes".

The eyes of foxes are well adapted to hunt during night time and they glow like green crystals when light is shone at them in darkness. The den of a fox is usually a burrow underground also referred as 'earth'. But they also live in cozy hollows above ground. Initially, the cubs learn the pounce technique used when hunting for prey. When bringing up pups, male foxes support the family by bringing food. When consuming food, foxes don't chew them. Instead, they cut them into chunks using their sharp teeth.

Foxes have retractable claws similar to cats. Their pupils are vertical and not rounded unlike other dogs. Since foxes have beautiful pelts, they are hunted for their fur by humans. Some farmers and game keepers have caught them using snares. However, fox hunting was banned under the Hunting Act in both Scotland and England during 2004 and 2006 respectively. Different species of foxes are found living in almost all continents.

# Characteristics

Foxes are usually small in size when compared with other members from the Canidae family such as jackals, domestic dogs and wolves. Female foxes are called vixens and they weigh slightly less than the males. Male foxes are known by the term of dogs, tods or reynards typically weighing around 5.9 kg on average. Foxes in the wild live up to 10 years but many of them survive only 2 or 3 years main causes being road accidents, hunting and diseases. Typical fox- like features include the presence of a bushy tail and a distinct muzzle. But other physical features depend on the habitat of a given species. For e.g., fox species adapted to a life in desert have short fur and large ears whereas fox species adapted to cold environments have thick, insulating fur with tiny ears.

Foxes do not live as packs every time. In fact, they live as small family units and hunt preys like rodents being opportunistic feeders. They use a pouncing technique to go for an easy kill. They also consume other sources of food such as small mammals, berries, grass hoppers etc. Two canine species having the ability to climb trees are the Gray Fox and the raccoon dog.

In Russia, a selective breeding program which lasted for around 45 years resulted in the production of a fox species known as silver fox. It was domesticated successfully. This research also gave rise to physical and behavioral traits that often appear in domestic cats, dogs and other animals.

# Foxes in different folklore and mythology

Red foxes were prominently featured in folklore and mythology of various human cultures. The Cadmean vixen or the Teumessian fox from the Greek mythology speaks about an enormous fox which was never destined to be caught. The red fox is considered as a symbolic animal in Celtic mythology. In order to steal butter from the neighbors, witches were thought to have taken the shape of foxes in the Cotswolds. Reynard the Fox in late European folklore symbolizes deceit and trickery. He appeared in the name of "Reinardus" originally.

In Korean folktales, fox spirits with nine tails are called 'kumiho' whereas in China, they are called 'huli jing'. Japanese mythology speaks about such spirits which are called 'kitsune' that possess magical abilities which increase with age and wisdom. The fox is deemed as cunning, deceitful, weak and a cowardly animal in Arab folklore faking its death by appearing bloated to pounce on an unsuspecting prey.

The pale fox was thought to be the desert's trickster God in dogon mythology. In ancient Peru, the Moche people used to worship animals. Foxes were used in their art. They believed that fox is a warrior who uses his mental power to fight without using physical attacks. Despite having the image of deceitfulness and cunningness in many cultures, foxes were considered sacred animals of goddess Ninhursag in early Mesopotamian mythology.

# Red Fox

The Red Foxes are considered to be the largest among true foxes. They are found living in Central America, Asia and Arctic Circle to North Africa. They were introduced to Australia which became a threat to native birds and mammals. Due to this very reason, they were enlisted among the "world's 100 worst invasive species". This species can adapt to new environments very quickly. Despite them being called "Red Fox", there are individuals with different colorations like melanises and albinos.

Red foxes are found usually in pairs or groups of families. Their main diet is small rodents. Apart from that, they consume young ungulates, reptiles, game birds, invertebrates and lipoids. Sometimes vegetables and fruits are taken too. They are vulnerable to attack from wolves, large sized felines, golden jackals and coyotes. They have been hunted extensively for their fur by humans.

They have a long, fluffy tail which reaches up to the ground in standing position. They are agile creatures having the ability of jumping over fences with more than 2 m in height. They are good swimmers too. Interestingly, they make use of their urine to mark their territories. They dig burrows in hills, bluffs, mountain slopes, ditches, gutters, ravines, and in human environments which are neglected. Red foxes make use of a vocal range during interaction. The sounds they produce could be divided into 2 as "Contact calls" and "Interaction calls". They prefer hunting in early morning hours before sunrise and late in the evening.

# Gray Fox

Many people tend to confuse Gray fox over Red fox because of their reddish brown fur in many parts of their body including chest, neck, ears, belly and feet. To add in, both look similar in size too. Male Gray foxes are slightly bigger in size than the females. These foxes are found in the southern region of North America starting from South of Canada to the northern area of South America. One time, they were found to be the most common fox in the east but human encroachment resulted in Red foxes being the dominant one. However, Gray foxes are dominant in Pacific states.

Rats, rabbits and mice are the main components in a Grey Fox's diet though they are omnivorous and include vegetables in their diet more than a red fox. They seldom raid on a farmer's henhouse. They are active at night and have a yapping bark.  One of the most interesting facts about them is that they are the only member of dog family capable of climbing trees.  The presence of hooked, non-retractable claws serve in providing a firm grip when climbing.  They do this to catch prey, escape from danger and to have a nap in a warm sunny day.  The lifespan of a wild Gray fox is 6-10 years on average.

# Arctic Fox

The Arctic fox is also known as the polar fox, white fox and snow fox. They are small in size native to the Arctic regions in the Northern hemisphere. Hence they are well adapted to cold environments. The body is round in shape to minimize the heat escaping from their body. Their thick fur appears white in winter and brown in summer. The diet of an Arctic fox consists of small animals such as voles, fish, ringed seal pups, learning and seabirds. They also consume seaweed, carrion and berries. They have furry paws which allow them to walk on ice when searching for food. They have a keen sense of hearing to locate the exact position of their prey under snow. After locating, they pounce and punch through the snow to get to their victim. If the hunted food is found to be abundant, they bury it and feast on it when food seems to be scarce.

Male Arctic foxes are slightly bigger than the females. There are two types of Arctic foxes living in Alaska. Blue and white. Blue Arctic foxes are grey and turn brown in summer. They are found in Southern mainland of Alaska and Aleutia. Their oily fur aids in repelling moisture from their body. White Arctic foxes are commonly found in Alaska. They look grey and brown in summer but appear snowy white in winter. Camouflage provides much needed protection for these creatures.

# Fennec Fox

Fennec fox is also known as the desert fox and is the smallest among all species. They are found in places where it is hot and dry such as deserts. Hence they are found in Sahara desert in North Africa and Asia. This fox has the ability to jump high in relation to their size which is really interesting.

They are cream or beige in colour which blends with their surroundings. Their tails are very long and has a black tip. The ears are easily recognizable due to its large size which helps to spread out heat and stay cool in hot deserts. It also helps to sense prey below the surface of the earth.

Fennec foxes hunt at night when the temperature is cooler. Though plants comprise a major portion of their diet, they also consume reptiles, birds, insects, small rodents and eggs. Hence they are omnivores. They can go on without water for long periods of time as they have adapted to such conditions in their environment. Potential predators of fennec foxes are hyenas, jackals, sulukis (an Egyptian domesticated dog) and caracals. However most surprisingly, eagle owl is the main predator.

Humans hunt fennec foxes for their soft fur and to keep them as pets since they are the only fox species which can be domesticated. Fennec foxes construct dens out of sand usually where plants are present for additional shelter. The average lifespan of a fennec fox in wild is 10 years whereas in captivity it can increase up to 12-14 years.

# Kit Fox

Kit foxes is a species found in North America. Their range mainly includes north and central Mexico as well as south western regions of America living throughout Nevada, Arizona, Utah, Western Texas and South eastern California. They have big ears which help them lower their body temperature much like fennec foxes. They can hear exceptionally well too. Male kit foxes are slightly bigger in size than the females. The body length varies between 455 to 535mm excluding the tail.

Kit fox's grey coat is accompanied with rusty tones. They have got no stripe along their tail unlike Gray Foxes. But however, they possess a tail with a black tip. The back has a darker shade than majority of their coat. The inner ears and belly have a lighter tone. Distinct dark patches surrounding the nose area is also a feature of kit fox.  They are mostly active at night but sometimes leave the den during daytime.  They usually hunt small animals like cottontail rabbits, hares, insects, fish snakes, dogs, meadow voles and prairie dogs.  If food becomes scarce, they opt for cactus fruits, tomatoes and other fruits.  Coyotes, red foxes bobcats, feral dogs and humans are predators of kit fox.  In order to stay warm in winter and cool during summer, kit foxes live in underground dens.

# Swift Fox

Swift foxes are closely related to kit foxes and sometimes considered as a subspecies of Vulpes velox because their hybrids are found naturally where ranges of both species overlap. They are the size of domestic cats and are native to the region of Great Plains in North America. However, they are found living in Colorado, Oklahoma, Montana, Texas and New Mexico. Though they neared extinction in the 1930s due to predator control programs, they were reintroduced successfully in later years.

Today, the IUCN (International Union for Conservation of Nature) has enlisted this species under Least Concern as stable populations are present elsewhere. Swift foxes are dark buffy grey in color with a tan yellow coloration in their legs and sides. The diet of a swift fox is mainly on birds, lizards, insects, rabbits, ground squirrels and mice. They have fruits and grasses too. Black patches are seen on their muzzles. Their tail has a black tip too. The ears are large which is quite noticeable. Males are bigger in size than the females. They are fast runners reaching speeds of over 30 mph or 40 mph. This is how they came to have their name as "Swift" fox. Badgers, bobcats and golden eagles are predators of Swift fox. But the main predator is coyote. Though less is known about the lifespan of a wild Swift fox, they are known to live up to 14 years in captivity.

# Bengal Fox

Indian fox, Vulpes bengalensis <u>Wikimedia Commons</u>

The Bengal fox is also called the Indian fox and as the name suggests, they are endemic to Indian subcontinent. Though they are found in much of the areas like the Himalayan foothills and southern or eastern Pakistan including Southeastern Bangladesh, they are not distributed in extreme arid zones or wet forests. They prefer to have scrub or thorn forests as their habitat avoiding tall grasslands with steep terrains.

Dens of Bengal foxes are complex with many chambers and escape routes. They hide themselves in subterranean dens or vegetation to escape from the heat of the day. Their diet consists of insects, reptiles, crabs, rodents, small birds, termites and fruits. Hence they are omnivores. These foxes are known to use a variety of vocalizations with pitch tones when communicating with one another. They can also bark, growl, whimper and whine.

The greatest threat to a Bengal fox is the lack of protection over their habitat. Wolves, feral dogs and humans are predators of this species. At present, there are no evidence to suggest these foxes are harmful to humans. But sadly in some regions, people consume their meat and use various parts of them in traditional medicines. Lifespan of an Indian fox is around 6 to 8 years in captivity though it can live up to 10 years in the wild.

# Silver Fox

Silver foxes are a species of red fox differentiated due to a color mutation. In other words, they are melanistic forms of red foxes some being bluish-grey, some totally black with a white lip on their tail while some others have a cinereous coloration on their sides. Silver foxes were most valued historically for their fur and the nobles in China, Russia and Western Europe wore their skin frequently. The long outer hair can grow up to 5 cm more than the shorter under fur present in various parts of the body such as the tail, behind the shoulders, under the throat and on sides. The hair is soft and glossy and has a reputation of being finer than pine morten. The fur present on the underbelly is finer while it is the shortest on limbs and forehead.

Silver foxes are widely distributed in the world. This could be due to their introduction to new habitats by humans for the purpose of fox hunting. 8% of red fox population in Canada comprise of silver foxes. The behaviors exhibited by silver foxes are very similar to the Red foxes. Scent marking is one such behavior. This is done to establish dominance, social records and to communicate about the availability of food in an area. Though they are omnivorous creatures, they prefer a carnivorous meal when meat becomes available. If meat becomes scarce, they depend heavily on plant matter. The Silver fox has featured several times in the society including totem poles.

# Crab-Eating Fox

Crab – Eating fox is endemic to the central region of South America.  They are also called the wood fox, common fox and forest fox.  They range in subtropical forests, shrubby thickets, woodlands, savannas and tropical savannas like plains, caatinga and campo in Colombia.  They are also found living in wooded river banks like the Riparian forest.  During dry periods, their habitat moves to low ground and in rainy season, it moves uphill.

Crab-eating Fox (*Cerdocyon thous*) from the Pantanal, Mato Grosso near Pousada Rio Claro <u>Wikimedia Commons</u>

The Crab-Eating fox is mainly greyish brown in color with red legs and face. Their ears and tails have a black tip. The legs are strong but short. However, the tails remains long and bushy. They usually weigh from 5-8 kilograms. The tail stands upright when they get excited. These animals are active at night and dusk. Dens dug by other animals are used by Crab-Eating foxes to spend their day. As the name suggests, they eat crabs. However, their diet also consists of birds, lizards, insects, eggs, fruits, tortoises and carrions.

Their pelt is not highly valued unlike other species. Hence they are hunted occasionally. They do not pose a threat to livestock. In fact, they really help in controlling harmful insects and rodents. Local people breed them often because these creatures are easy to domesticate. Though they live in pairs, hunting is done alone. Wide variety of body languages and vocalizations are used as a means of communication.

# South American Gray Fox

The South American Gray Fox is known by several names such as Chilla, Patagonian fox and Grey Zorro. They live in the Southern Cone of South America, especially in chilli and Argentina. They inhabit the western semi-arid regions of Argentina and throughout chilli including the Atacama Desert. In late 1920s and early 1930s, this species was introduced to the Falkland Islands. Even today, they can be found in large numbers on Weddell Islands, Beaver and smaller islands. The habitat of a South American gray fox is seen on forest edges, plains, foothills of mountain ranges and grasslands of Southern South America.

The body length of a South American Gray fox ranges between 42 to 68 cm and they weigh around 2 to 4 Kgs. They have got no subspecies. Their coat is grey in color with pale grey under parts. They possess long bushy tails and large eyes. Markings of rust coloration are found around their legs, head and ears. They are endothermic animals. That is, they have to generate their own heat to maintain body temperature. The diet of this species changes seasonally. They are omnivores with a diet consisting of small mammals, fruits, frogs, bird eggs, scorpions, insects, seeds, berries, frogs and lizards. One misconception people have about these foxes has let these creatures to be called as 'lamb killers'. However it should be noted that they kill lambs very rarely maybe just to survive during draught. There have been no documentation about the predators of South American Gray Fox.

# Bat-Eared Fox

The Bat- Eared fox is also known as the cape fox, big eared fox, Delalande's fox and black eared fox.  They are found living in arid regions of savannah and short grasslands.  However, 2 different populations of this species are found in Africa.  Bat eared foxes are named most probably after the Egyptian slit faced fruit bat which also had large ears.  In recent studies it is revealed that Bat- Eared foxes are closely related to true foxes.  This species was widely distributed during the Pleistocene era.

The teeth of a Bat- Eared Fox are quite small and perfectly adapted for an insectivorous diet.  Their main food is harvester termites.  If this termite species is not available, they go for other species of termites or insects like ants, beetles, moths, spiders, millipedes and grasshoppers. However, reptiles, wild berries, rodents and small snakes also form a part of their diet. Hence they play a major role in controlling termites. It is estimated that a single Bat-Eared Fox can consume up to 1.5 million termites every year. Now that is a huge amount.

Bat- Eared Foxes are quite fast and good at dodging. They flee to their dens when faced with a danger from predators. Rock pythons, leopards, jackals, African wild dogs, cheetah and spotted hyenas are their predators. Their ears help them a great deal in listening to the sounds made by insects underground. It is really interesting to note that these creatures use tail posture as well as facial expressions apart from olfactory signals and vocalizations to communicate with one another. During summer, harvester termites become their main source of food while on winter, different ant species become their food.

# Hoary Fox

Uma raposa domesticada no interior do Ceará <u>Wikimedia Commons</u>

Hoary Fox is also referred as Hoary Zorro and small toothed dog. They are a native species to south central Brazil living in bush lands, woodlands and mountainous savannah territories. Hoary foxes are grey in color with light under body. Their ears and legs appear reddish. "Hoary" literally means white. Hence they get this name due to the white markings on their coat.

Some individuals are melanistic. Hoary foxes are small in size weighing only about 3 to 4 kg. Its slender body form makes it a fast and an agile creature.

Diet of a Hoary fox consists mainly of insects such as termites, grasshoppers and small invertebrates. Their teeth are small and well adapted to this kind of diet. They also consume small birds, fruits and rodents when available. These animals are active during night time. According to the Red List of IUCN (International Union for Conservation of Nature), Hoary foxes are enlisted under Data Deficient category since an assessment on its risk of extinction cannot be made directly or indirectly due to the lack of adequate information on these species. However, the Management Plant and the Canid Conservation Assessment has listed these creatures under 'vulnerable'.

Hoary foxes are known to attack poultry occasionally. They also carry many diseases that can be transmitted to humans and domestic dogs.

# Tibetan Sand Fox

An illustration of a Tibetan fox Alere Flammam. 1890
<u>Wikimedia Commons</u>

Tibetan Sand Fox is commonly known as Sand fox or Tibetan fox in simple

terms.  But this terminology could be confusing as the Corsac Fox, another fox type is also known by these terms. Tibetan sand foxes are small in size having soft and dense coats. Their muzzles are narrow. Flanks, cheeks, rumps and upper legs of a Tibetan sand fox are grey. However, their bucks, necks, muzzles, crowns and lower legs are tan and rufous in color. Their tails are bushy with white tips. They have short ears. An adult fox weigh around 4 to 5.5 kg on average. They possess canine teeth which are longer than a hill fox's.

Tibetan sand foxes are found in Tibetan Plateau and Ladkh Plateau. Apart from that, they are also found outside China in northern Bhutan and in the borders of India and Nepal. The habitats of this species are usually found away from any human contact and heavy vegetation. They are solitary creatures and hunt during daytime. Their diet mainly consists of rodents, pikas, lizards, woolly hares and marmots. They also scavenge on carcasses of blue sheep, Tibetan antelopes, musk deer and livestock. Interestingly, they pair up with brown bears when hunting for pikas. These creatures help in contributing towards the control of small animals and rodent population. Unlike some other species, they are not hunted extensively for pelts as their fur has a minor value.

# Author Bio

Rachel Smith is a young author who enjoys animals. She's always wanted to get a both a guinea pig and a rabbit and have them live together. Once, she had a rabbit that was very nervous, and chewed through her leash and tried to escape. She's also had several pet mice, which were the funniest little animals to watch. She lives in Ohio with her family and writes in her spare time.

## Download Free Books!

## http://MendonCottageBooks.com

Purchase at Amazon.com

Website http://AmazingAnimalBooks.com

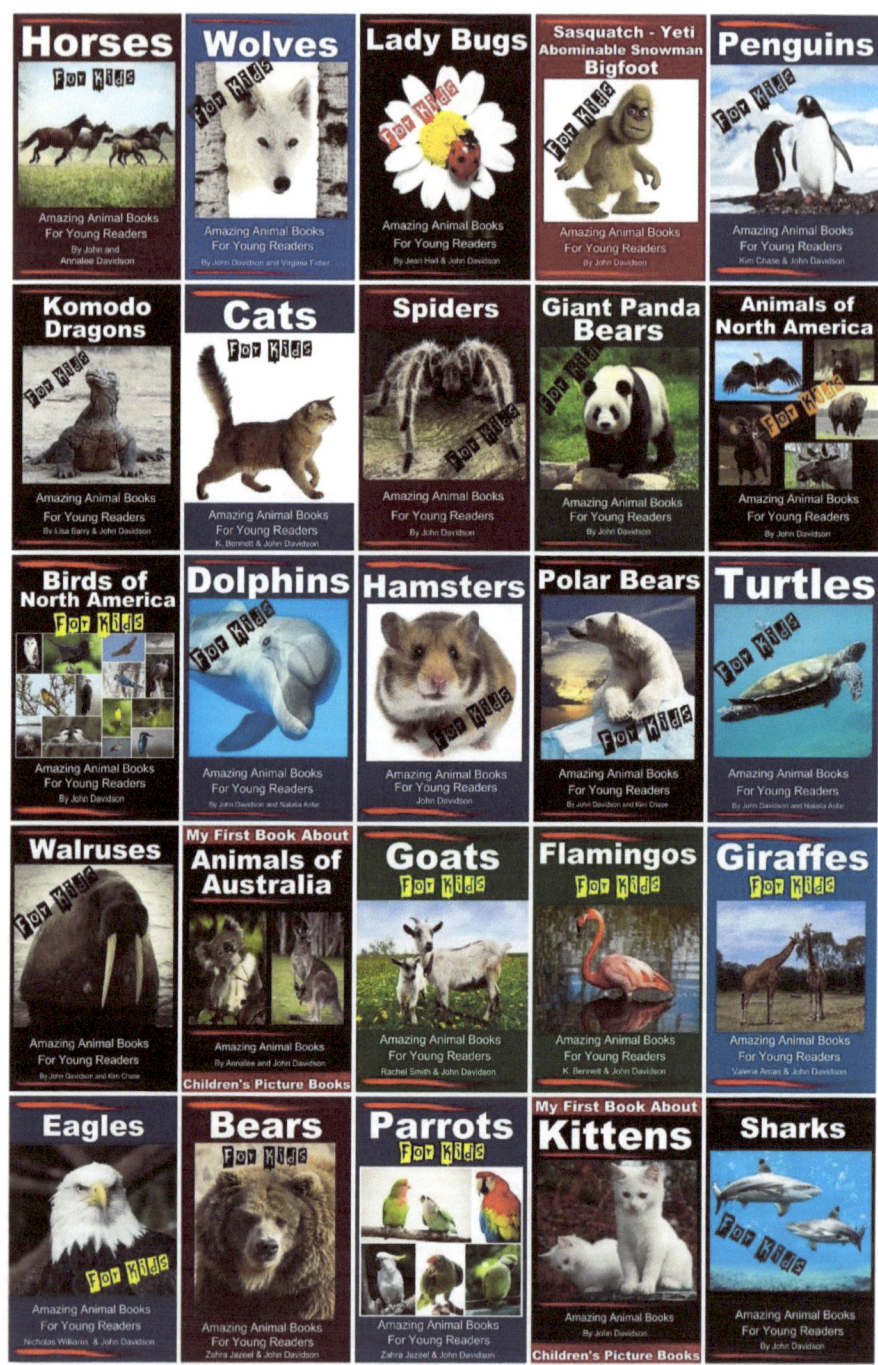

Our books are available at


1. Amazon.com

2. Barnes and Noble

3. Itunes

4. Kobo

5. Smashwords

6. Google Play Books


# Download Free Books!

# http://MendonCottageBooks.com

# Publisher

JD-Biz Corp

P O Box 374

Mendon, Utah 84325

http://www.jd-biz.com/

Mendon Cottage Books

P O Box 374, Mendon Utah 84325

www.ingramcontent.com/pod-product-compliance
Lightning Source LLC
Chambersburg PA
CBHW050840290526
45792CB00001B/474